For Craig,

I know Mummy would be very pleased

you have a copy.

With her and my love

Katrina.

THIS IS THE MORNING OF MY LIFE

A Garland of Poems

KRISTIN MacEwan

This is the Morning of my Life – a Garland of Poems
by Kristin MacEwan

All Rights Reserved. Copyright © Kristin MacEwan 2011

Published by Katriona MacEwan

Selection and editorial copyright © Katriona MacEwan 2011
Photographs copyright © Katriona MacEwan, Duncan MacEwan 2011
Art copyright © Niall McWilliam 2007, 2008

Edited by Katriona MacEwan
Designed by Jo Digby, *north & south design*

ISBN: 978-0-9569931-0-6

Printed by Meigle Colour Printers Ltd., Galashiels 2011
Bound in hardback by Hunter & Foulis, Edinburgh 2011

This book is being sold in aid of pkd charity

contents

This book is dedicated with all
my love to my Mother
Ann Kristin MacEwan.

I hope it will bring joy to my Daddy,
Duncan MacEwan and my three
sisters Fiona, Rosalind and Andrea.

May it lift the spirit of every reader
who turns its pages.

All profits from the sale of this book are being
donated to the Polycystic Kidney Disease Charity.

If you wish to purchase further copies, please email:
kmacewan@btinternet.com
or you can order online at www.pkdcharity.org.uk.

Introduction by Katriona MacEwan

Kristin MacEwan was my Mother. Towards the end of her life, she decided she wanted to create an anthology of all the poems she'd written. She had long held a dream of publishing her own book.

Kristin had polycystic kidney disease (PKD) and was on dialysis as a result of renal failure for the last 8 years. I was involved with poetry and publishing during my BBC career and before she died, Mummy asked me to edit and publish her work, and that is why this book has been created.

The format is semi-autobiographical as I encouraged Mummy to write introductions to individual poems and a significant part of her life story is re-told throughout. I believe this makes the book quite unique. Kristin's introductions are printed in italics alongside her photograph. I have also written some narrative and my words appear in a coloured-shaded margin.

I decided that "The Seasons" would be a strong theme to bind the poems together, as Mummy loved nature so much. Amazingly, her creative hand has somehow been across the whole process. One day, as I was beginning to group the poems, I opened her old Rudolf Steiner exercise book, only to discover that the very same quotes I had chosen were illustrated in the centre pages in her own handwriting! The poems are clustered together and linked to each other, either by their subject matter, or the date when they were originally written.

The photographs come from the MacEwan family photo albums, the landscapes are exclusively of the Scottish Borders where I live and Loch Lomond (a place Mummy loved). A great many of them have a special significance to the family. The striking artwork used throughout the book, is by a talented artist from Edinburgh, called Niall McWilliam.

Mummy wanted this anthology to be a "Garland of Poems" and the garland artwork has been painted by her grandchild Hannah.

Enabling my Mother's dream to come true, has been a creative challenge and a great honour.

Mummy wanted a copy of this book to be in every dialysis Unit in the United Kingdom; so whoever may be reading this, may her poetry uplift your spirit and bring joy to your soul.

The news that I was to be on haemodialysis for the rest of my life simply shattered me. This sort of thing just didn't happen to me, but it did, and it has. But when you think about it, it's a bonus, a beautiful golden eight precious years of seeing my daughter re-married, and my grandchildren grow more beautiful each day. So I greet each morning as a gift, a new day, the morning of my life.

This is the Morning of My Life

This is the morning of my life
Be still and watch a star-drenched sky
Herald dawn with soaring music,
As drifts of swallows soar and fly.

Stretching forth I reach the sunshine –
Source of life and warmth and growth,
New power again and rising glory,
Golden rays that seek the truth.

Daylight rushes forth from darkness,
Life force powers the world anew.
I am here to greet this moment,
And my breath drinks deep the hue.

Bless me Father this new morning,
Take my hand but let me stay,
Be my guide and comfort ever
As I step into the day.

*Published by Forward Press in January, 2010
in their anthology entitled "UK Inspirations"*

"A host of golden daffodils" WORDSWORTH

A few snowdrops:

Once upon a time in an old Keep in the depths of Aberdeenshire a baby girl was born. Her name was Kristin. It was the 7th of May 1932 when she was thrust into the world in a heavy snowstorm. Snow is lucky. I am lucky and most fortunate. That child was me.

May

How Joyous is the month of May
That month that I was born,
The hawthorn with its rich display
Pays homage to the dawn.

A cuckoo calls with rhythmic voice
A new day has begun.
As daffodils and primroses
Turn to reach the sun.

The world around is burgeoning
With life and blossoms new,
As nature breathes again with joy
Meadows are drenched with dew.

The sound of living fills the air
As giddy bees begin to fly,
And floating clouds with patchwork-blue
Do paint a shining sky.

How cold can be the month of May,
For in a valley deep and white
A lake began to freeze one night
That was the time when I was born
In the midst of a silent snowstorm.

Published by Forward Press in their "Contributors'
Collection - A Moment To Muse" 2010

Spring

Running through the meadow
Running through the grass,
Buttercups and cowslips
Bursting brimming gold;
Reflections of bright new sunshine
Breaking through the winter's cold.

Golden hair brushed by the wind
Blows gently round her face.
Earth and sky surround her
In this time and space.

The air is filled with birdsong now
Singing, ringing through the trees,
That shudder with the touch of spring
Awakening to the breeze.

Running up the mountainside
The summit is so clear,
The sight from here is breathtaking
At this time of year.

When winter folds away its cold
And spring is almost here
Now listen to the single bell
That echoes through the valley.

God is with us on this day
High upon the hill
Stretch out your hand and touch him
And you can hear his voice
For Eastertide is nearly here
Rejoice again, Rejoice!

Written March 2002

Angels Wings

I need the sun on my face and the bold earth strong beneath my feet
I need the wind in my hair
I need a hand to hold me gently
I need love to surround me
I need the frothing sea at my feet
I need the sand between my toes
I need my golden daughters to lift my spirits high
I need the sun in the morning and the moon at night
I need my beloved husband just to be there
I need angel nurses to help me get strong
I need my star to guide me and show me the way.

Mummy wrote this poem to celebrate her 70th Birthday, she adored a party and having all the family together round the table, including the grandchildren. We all enjoyed a wonderful dinner party in an elegant room at Lumley Castle and she read this out loud to us all.

Family Celebration

You are just incredible
My miracles divine.
You are simply lovely,
And what's more
You are mine.

Your love surrounds me
Each morning bright
And what's more mes enfants
Your gear is out of sight!

I adore each one of you
In my own special way.
But honestly my family,
What more can I say
But thank you for this
My perfect day!

Written to celebrate Kristin's 70th Birthday
7th May 2002

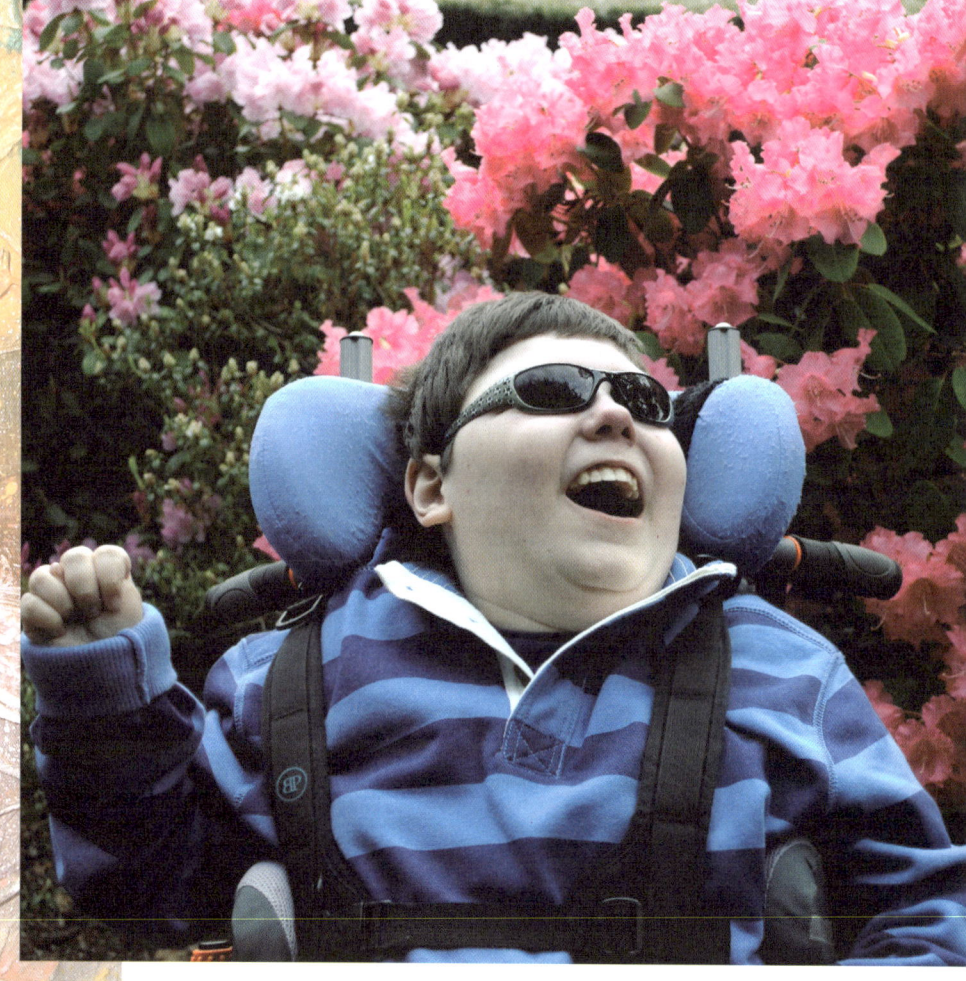

My grandson was very seriously ill in Great Ormond Street Hospital, we stood by his bed praying, and felt that he would not be too long in this world. For three nights I didn't sleep. One night I got up at about 2 o'clock in the morning and wrote this poem in anticipation of the tragedy I feared could be about to strike us. Matthew is very strong and he survived. Today he is a beautiful, sunny child, who is still very much with us. Matthew was born in May like me.

For Matthew

Do not stand by my bed and weep
I am not there.

I am the still air that touches your cheek,
I am the ground under your feet,
A singing lark that soars in flight.
I am not here, but just out of sight.

I am the rain that drenches your hair
In a meadow high with grass.
This pain will pass.
A tambourine rattle, a burst of Bach,
The tide at my feet now,
A wave in my hand, the rush of the sand.

All these things I love are here
Do not despair, do not fear,
For my wings are strong now.
I can see the sun,
The morning is bright now,
I am having fun.
My journey's almost done.

Written 15th April 1999

I have a very dear friend who was struggling at a time in her life. A "sort of madness" happened around her and she lost direction. I wrote these few words to calm her and she has treasured them, and now is her old self again: bright and beautiful.

A Morsel of Love

Do not fly too fast little bird,
You will dash against the glass
And that would be absurd, little bird
As all the sky is your window.

Soar with even wings
And sing in the firmament,
Dip and dive, trill land thrive,
Fly safely little bird, stay alive.

Written February 2002

I have wondered about this poem, whether it is a fantasy poem or based on reality. Kristin had four daughters, and seven grandchildren. When the first boy grandchild appeared, it was quite something in our family! His name was Philip. I have wondered if this poem may have been inspired by his birth.

Friday's Child

Now my babe is here at last
The fears and yearning gone.
He wakes each sleepy midnight,
And cries each waking dawn.

So close to me, so fragile
I hold him next to my heart,
His fingers tight around my own
Please God we never part.

My small cocoon of wonder
Held closely on my breast.
A tiny bluebird heaven sent
Safe in a woolly nest.

My soul doth magnify the Lord
With ecstasy and joy
For like my sister Mary mild
I have my baby boy.

Kristin's mother was Elinor Rainy, she died on 1st March 1966, aged 66. Mummy never got over the loss of her Mother throughout her life, she had loved her so very deeply. I never knew that she had called her "Mama", until I read this. This poem is a very poignant picture of Grandmother Rainy.

For Mama

When I think of Mama
Most of all I remember
Her hazel eyes so deep and clear,
Her laughter bright as morning sunshine,
Her long cascading chestnut hair.

Her slender arms so strong around me,
Somehow she was always there.
Her silken hands that played the piano,
The music gloriously filled the air.
Her mind so keen and sharp
It sought the answers.
She had such elegance, such flair.

My friend for life, she gave me mine.
My guiding star, my comfort in the dark,
Her wisdom shone like a bright white light,
She handed me my spark.

Her love for me was infinite
I feel it with me still.
I remember Mama
And I always will.

I gave Mummy a hard back notebook, and told her that if she felt inspired or wanted to help the time in hospital go faster, she could always write a poem.

Amazingly this was written on 9th May 2006 – whilst she was actually attached to the machine receiving dialysis.

Heaven and Hell

What is Heaven?
Is there a Hell?

Heaven is …
Waking at dawn's early light
And watching as it drenches my room
My dear blue room,
Chasing the night and dispelling the gloom.
Heaven is hearing the birds chirruping,
To carol the morning and welcome the Spring.
To waken the sky with terrestrial light
Dispelling the dark and dread of night.
The dawn and its powers come rushing in
And surround me with calm.
This is peace, this is Heaven,
A Jerusalem balm.

Hell is …
Trapped on a bed with a broken wing
Joined to a giant, a great thundering thing
That snarls and grumbles and gurgles and,
Tries to bring comfort and new life and make you feel well.
It's more like Heaven really, than it is like Hell.

Kind faces surround me,
Angel nurses are there,
Their hands hold me tightly so there's nothing to fear.
Their laughter's infectious,
I begin to smile
And drift off a moment to sleep for a while.

Flying home is Heaven,
Simply Heaven on earth.
Silver wings that are strong with regenerated birth.
Warm arms now surround me
And make me feel whole
Thank you dear Heaven
For that day that I stole.

Places

Places to be
Places to see
Places to pray
Places to say, I love you.
Places to die,
Where angels fly.
Places to be born
Places where you lie in the corn.

Places far away
Places to stay
Places to lie in the sun
Places to sing
Places to bring loved ones to.

A place by the sea
A place you can just be
And gather pebbles on the beach
Finding bright Easter eggs hiding just out of reach.
A place to be ill
A place to be still and smell the blossom.

So many places to be in the world
And so many places to roam.
But the very best place in all the world
Is the place that is most loved
The place that I call home.

Written on 21st April 2006

Seeing is Believing

It happened in a garden,
A garden filled with joy.
It happened to a girl,
It happened to a boy.
They ate the apple on that tree
And swiftly fell from grace.
They were banished from that garden,
That perfect wondrous place.
They were banished into darkness,
And could not see their face.

They were drawn into knowledge
And smothered in its spell.
They fell from heaven that day,
In through the gates of hell.
They lay there on their tree of thorns
In despair and pain.
Their perfect life in paradise
Never to see again.

They bore their brood in mud and fear,
And thought that they were free.
They lived together in that place,
In strife and agony.
They saw the apple on that tree,
But never again God's face.

Seeing but not believing is their own tragic loss
One day, God's son will walk on earth
And hang upon a cross.

Written on 21st May 2005

This was one of the last poems I think Mummy may have written, as it was found under her pillow after she died in May 2010. It shows her longing and love of nature so much. It seems just like a conversation she may have had with her young granddaughter Beatrice. I sense Mummy's fragility very much in this poem. She was born in the Spring and died in the Spring. How the circle of life forms and meets in the middle in these words.

A few snowdrops

The Last Spring

When is Spring coming again Grandma?
The snow has nearly faded away
We really need some sun
To make the flowers grow and stay.

I love the snowdrops on the bank
And want to pick them all.
They are so lovely to me
But Mama says if you pick them all
There'll be nothing more to see next year.

Perhaps the primroses will grow to
Fill our hearts with joy.
And then we can go for walks in the sun,
And shoo the snow away.

Please tell me now that Spring has come
Dear Grandma dear, and that it's here to stay.

Mr. Wordsworth said

What does poetry mean to you?
Pretty words to soothe the soul.
Or tormented tirades of anguish
Prose to make someone else whole.

What is poetry truly?
Reflections on eternity and life
Yet seen through a glass darkly
And echoed through eons of strife.

Wordsworth's clouds and daffodils
Somehow make our hearts rejoice -
That such a man in such a way
Could speak with such a voice.

Through him the world doth come alive,
The mind is filled with clarity,
The eyes are opened, the breathing calm,
We sense a true polarity.

What is poetry honestly?
Truth upon paper put,
So that others may dream what you can dream
And grow from that same root.

Poetry is the quintessence of life itself.
A spilling over of joyous emotion,
A falcon in flight of feathered motion.
The singing of a bird
Poetry is true happiness
The creation of the word.

When they moved to Hemel Hempstead, Mummy joined a Poetry Group, run by Jean Stevens of St. John's Parish Church. They regularly met on a on a Friday afternoon. This group inspired her to begin to write more and to learn about different poetic styles and techniques. This is a tribute to all of them.

The Friday People

We sit in a stable and share with each other
The joys and despair of each sister and brother.
The sadness within us dispels with the morning
Replaced by new daybreak – thought which is dawning.

There are angels in Times Square that herald and sing
And there's Charles on his mountain saluting his King.
His Lord re-discovered, a light in his dark.
Golden angels are singing in MacArthur Park.

Now a child's eyes are closing, now a missing gold link,
Jean's pen on her paper, it does make us think.
There are memoirs of mothers, and memorials to life,
Children, prayers and sweet sunshine, and a trip on a bike.

Now that saga Silvania continues with Anne,
Who hates being a spy, but will she lay her man?
The mystery, the madness – it goes on for ever,
And encouraged by Hilda we're ever so clever.

Those angels still singing, they know what to say,
Walk with us sweet stranger on this Christmas Day.
But through all of our searching you listen serene,
Our mentor, our mother, our literacy queen.

So shine for us Hilda, inspire us still more,
So that each of us here, now, can open that door
To all that is wondrous within us, and new
To all that is tortured, to all this is true.

Those angels still singing? They're here with us now
They're singing for joy and then telling us how
We can do so much better, we can stretch out so far.
We can give to tomorrow and follow it's star.

So let's ring out that carol
Echo turret and steeple.
Let's keep writing for joy,
We're the good Friday people.

A creative friend of Mummy's- Katrina Graham, decided to set up a small poetry group in Boxmoor of her own. Six enthusiastic poets met for the first time in Spring 2005, including Mummy and I. Initially we started by reading published poets out loud on a specific theme, but the whole purpose was to create our own poetry and to encourage each other. We were challenged to write something new each month. During the five years she took part in it, Mummy wrote some of her best work, it was often the highlight of her week especially when she became very ill. This ditty is a tribute to Poetry Power, sent with Mummy's love to Katrina, Keith, John and Frances.

A New Beginning

A single step with hearts that are free
A genesis for us to see
A first moment
A first time
A new beginning to learn about rhyme
An old door slams shut
And a new door opens
A renaissance ready to flower
Ready to think, and ready to fly
Six souls learning poetry power.

Written February 2005

Sometimes as a writer when you look at a blank page and cannot see anything, you feel you've got "writer's block" then suddenly the ideas start to flow and you discover that there is a poem there!

A Blank Page

What are you doing girl?
What do you need to say?
There is no time to waste dear,
Make it work today!
Just get on with it girl
And write the damn thing down.

Write a single sentence,
And make it come to life.
Work with your pen and paper
And cut it like a knife.
Bring in all your gladness,
Even sadness
Bring it all to life.

Write a movie, make it strong.
Write a poem and make it a song.
Make it powerful, make it fine
Then you can say ....
"That poem is mine".

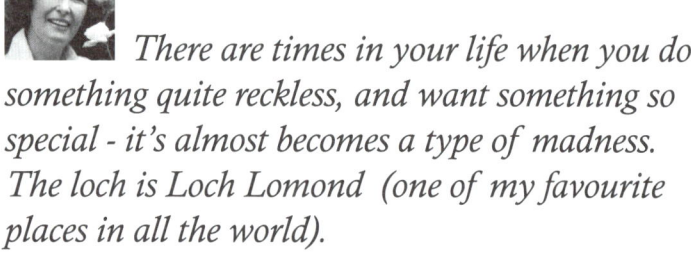

There are times in your life when you do something quite reckless, and want something so special - it's almost becomes a type of madness. The loch is Loch Lomond (one of my favourite places in all the world).

On this occasion I found the temptation too great!

A Bit of Bling

I saw it in the window
Shining white against the sun
I had to have it,
I needed to have it
Before the day was done.

I need the air to breathe
And a lark singing on high.
I need the rain upon my face
And wings so I can fly.

I need sun in the morning
And the moon at night.
I need to see a silken loch
Painted silver with light.
I need your arms around me
Deep into the night.

I love being on earth
And I do love to fly.
It's just like this I suppose
Sometimes you really need a fling
It is a sort of madness
That makes your heart sing.

So
I walked into the shiny shop
And bought a bit of bling!

Absolute Nonsense

It's funny to be funny
To make some people laugh.
It can be really easy
It can be really hard.
To smile is just so loving
It lightens up the day,
And when you smile
It don't matter really what you have to say.
You can say something that's stupid

You can say something that's wise,
As long as you are smiling
It brightens up your eyes.

So let's try to be more happy
And lighten up each day.
Let's be careful when we speak
And what we want to say.
Be kindly and be loving
And not just for a while,
So that every time we see a friend
We great them with a smile.

Written 12th September 2005

summer

"My **luve's** like a **red red rose**" BURNS

I saw him across a crowded room. Every time I looked at him he was looking at me. When he turned his head I was looking at him. It certainly was … "One enchanted evening you will see a stranger across a crowded room …".

I had been invited by the Principal of the Diaghilev Exhibition at the Edinburgh Art College to join him. I was in the process of being trained as a presenter for TV (yes, they did train people in those good old days!), having just got back hot foot from Paris, where I had been studying for 9 months with Pierre Bernac (A French Baritone). I had so wanted to follow my dream in the footsteps of the opera singer Maria Callas. In Edinburgh I was considered for the Kathleen Ferrier Award, but in Paris I soon knew that I was not going to be good enough to survive on an international stage; and I don't do failure!

I have to say, to get back to the story, that Duncan got himself introduced to me. In those days it wasn't 'Here fellows, there's lassies, let's mingle'! Duncan, for that was his name, invited me very formally to lunch.

Each day of my life has been an infinite joy to be together, I wrote this poem for him on our Golden Wedding Anniversary, and I was so delighted when Forward Press published it in "Love's Many Mysteries" anthology in 2009.

We were married on 1st of June 1956 in St. Mary's Cathedral, Edinburgh. Game, set and match, 53 years of marriage later our love affair continues …

Just for the Love of Duncan

How many ways do I love thee?
More than I can ever say.
For the moment I saw you was my moment
Across a crowded room, your clear blue eyes
Looked up at me and loved me that first second,
My whole being in that moment came alive.

That moment at the altar was my moment.
My heartbeat drowned the organ, would I cry?
I am yours and you are mine now
Yes Beloved,
For better or for worse now till we die.

Lying in your arms must be my moment.
Harmony together, you and I.
Could there ever be again that perfect moment?
Joyous love and starlight shining from your eyes.

The first of our four daughters was my moment.
New pain transfused to joy and raucous cries.
They're wrapped within my arms, my lovely babies
Looking at me with their father's eyes.

Every morning I see you is our moment.
Each day, new joy beginning, new surprise.
I love you now, and always will remember
The first time that I looked into your eyes.

Written June 2006

Golden

Your ring upon my finger
Your golden ring of mine
You shine as summer morning
You glow as summer wine.

Mine is the joy and the gladness
With heart a flutter, free as a dove.
Suddenly one Summer you were there
And as suddenly we were in love.

Sea birds calling, diving and falling
Heart to heartbeat and sky.
Bodies of salt, sea and sunshine
Golden arms, golden rings, golden thigh.

Thundering waves and our laughter
Salt sea and wild geese that fly.
Bodies that are burnished in sunshine
Golden people in love, you and I.

You don't need to ask any grandparent how it feels when the grandchildren are coming to stay for the Summer holiday. Everything has to be spick and span, the lawn mowed, the cats groomed, fresh linen on the beds, and the flowers all looking wonderful. The house where we lived at that time used to creak with anticipation!

Half an hour after the entourage had arrived, the whole place was looking as though a hurricane had hit it, but joy was infinite, the joy to have the little ones encircle you with their arms and say "Hello Grandma, I missed you". A great start to the Summer holiday.

Sudden Sun

Our home comes alive with laughter and fun,
The grandchildren are on their way.
The old house yawns in the morning sun,
The young ones are coming to stay.

The cats all groomed and puckered up,
Are purring with delight
Prepared to leap up the nearest tree
When our granddaughter gives them a fright!

"There's the horn, they're in the drive –
They're here!" I call "Let's hurry!"
Doors fly open, hearts turn over,
Two worried cats scurry.

"Hi Grandma! Hi Popsi"
Hello darlings, you're here!"
"Oh Mamsi, what a journey!"
"Welcome dearest, welcome dear".

Hearts near stopping, kissing softness.
"How you've grown my little one"
Blue eyes shining, arms entwining,
"Welcome daughter, welcome son."

Rushing footsteps, utter turmoil
Instant happiness begun.
Fairytales and looking glasses
Nappies blowing in the sun.

All our children are together,
The old house smiles in the noon-day sun.
It loves the hustle, the hassle, the hubbub,
The Summer holiday has begun.

What Do I See?

I see a wave rushing towards me, frothing and white

I see my reflection in a tranquil pool filled with sea anemones

I see the sand, soft between my toes

I see the yellow gorse shuddering with a rush of wind

I see the clouds drifting white across the sky

I see the moon disappear

I see the sun burning out of the sea

I see my family joyfully trudging over the dunes,
Waving and laden with baskets filled with goodness
For the glorious day ahead

I see me happy, happy, surrounded by my golden girls.

This poem was written nearly 4 years before Mummy died, but it shows how she felt she was often really on the edge of life, struggling to survive.

The Breath of Life

Breathing, breathing, breathing life
Bursting through our burning hearts.
Breath on windows burnt with ice
Breaking ice that cools the blood.
Blood on ice when breath has gone.
Stillness then
A silent song.

Seeing eyes of single tears
That cry and cry to bring again
That breath of life,
That urgent single sigh.
I turn to see my breath on glass
This time I did not die.

Written on 30th July 2006

Peace

Peace is being still
Peace is listening to the silence
Peace is watching the grass grow.
Peace is that sigh as your baby falls asleep in your arms.

Peace is lying in the heather and
Listening to a skylark soaring above.
Peace is in the mountains drifting close around you
As the day gets gently swallowed by night.

The peace of God that passes all understanding
That sacred peace within you
I listen in the silence and feel calm.

The Indian Summer Sun

How many ways can I tell you
Of the glory and beauty of that day.
The Indian Summer Sun swam around us
Cocooning us in its warmth and light.

The laden pear and apple trees
Heavy with their burden for harvest
Swayed gently
 In a Southerly breeze.

The haven of the luscious garden
An oasis in a mad world
Surrounded us
With its tranquillity and peace.

Drinking champagne on the lawn
Wearing wide straw hats and panamas
Birdsong bright in our ears
My senses stirred by sumptuous food
Under a canopy of cream calico.

Such a day to remember
Such perfection
Joyfully spent in the loving company
Of my very best friend.

Written after a glorious Summer lunch
with Jennifer on September 15th 2007.

It was an amazing day! The sun was blazing down on us. We had been given the honour of having a summer lunch with the Queen at Buckingham Palace, to commemorate 60 years after the end of World War II.

My husband was in India for 2 years from 1945 – 1947, and he and those other such wonderful men were honoured, and invited to some marvellous occasions during a week of celebration. They were also invited to return to the place they were stationed in the war, so my husband went back to India with one of our daughters. He had a very moving journey, with all the dust and heat and smells of that country, and fell in love with India all over again.

Well to get back to the Palace, as it were! We were seated at round tables. Ours was for the Royal Signals, and our lovely Queen was at the next table, with the Duke of York on the other side.

But the picture that stays bright in my memory still, was the Queen on the balcony after lunch with millions of poppy petals floating down around her. The sky was filled with old Hurricane planes that shed the petals into the air, turning a golden sun, blood red.

It was a most powerful and moving image and so I took up my pen to try to capture it in words.

We Will Remember Them

People are here to remember.
Blood red poppies floating free
Each petal a precious life gone.
Uplifted faces searching the sky,
Bright tears unshed held in the sunshine.
Too much to remember.

Skies filled with bombs night after night
Rubble everywhere, buildings buried.
Sleeping in Anderson shelters and
Underground, dark and cold.
Wardens perched on the roof-tops
Scanning the black sky.

ALL CLEAR!

Breathing again, now we can rest.
Fathers and sons fighting far, far away,
In deserts, in jungles, in drenching heat.
Mothers now land girls, ploughing the fields
And "Digging for Victory"!
Children huddled together in the steam
And dust of a waiting train,
A gas mask hanging on narrow shoulders.
Clinging to a label and their mother's hand,
That hand so loving, now coarse and rough
From working on the factory floor,
Making weapons to end all wars.
No news, no letters, no telegram – "THANK GOD!"
Broken hearts, broken bodies, all broken.

The poppies still tremble, red in the sky.
We will remember them, oh yes we will remember.

Written 31st July 2005

Written for my daughter at a time when she was in great sadness and despair.

Holy Water

The day the rains came down
She stood upon that hill.
The water swept across her brow,
Her eyes were closed and still.

The heavens wept and so did she
So silently forlorn.
She mourned her life and one dead child,
She mourned each waking dawn.

Like trunk of tree she stood
So still, so silent, somehow waiting.
The rain continued endlessly,
Cloud bursting unabatedly.

The willows bent in harmony
From water into water.
Their silver bows entwined
Outstretched, like mother greeting daughter.

Come womankind, open your eyes
And see what is about.
Such beauty in a weeping world
Wake up, stop having doubt.

Gird up your loins with joy again
And step into the morning.
Stop feeling sad and fearful
The new day must be dawning.

Then you must look out not in,
To where the desert earth
Begins again to multiply
With spiritual re-birth.

Come down sweet rain from Heaven above
Refresh her arid soul with love.
Allow him in and flower anew.
Come woman, mother, it is you!
You're not immortal, you're not divine.
Come mother earth, drink deep his wine.

It was the time of the Edinburgh Festival and as a Studio Manager in BBC Radio, I was assigned to edit the play "Under Milk Wood" by Dylan Thomas, for the Kaleidoscope Programme.

Richard Burton had made a simply stunning recording of the play, bringing the whole story alive with his rich, dark tones. I was deeply moved and perhaps there is a little of Dylan somewhere in this next piece.

The Festival of Dawn

The still sound of silence that trembles in the air,
A single bell, a dog that barks,
A distant cockerel crowing,
Gradually the orchestra of morning slowly growing.

The festival of dawn begun,
The thrusting rush of rising sun,
The fierce and fiery glow transforms
The sky with liquid light.
The world begins to breathe anew,
And wakens from the night.

But still the waiting silence deep
As shrouded houses silent sleep,
Then a single sound would quiver,
Sending up wild geese that shiver
Into fiery dawn,
Chorusing another morn.

A single star through rain washed grey
Gives welcome to another day.
Again the urgent cockerel crows
And children huddle under bedclothes
And babies cry and lovers sigh.

The silence simply melts away,
And night capitulates to day.

Written September 1999
Published by Forward Press in their
Lyrical Winds, Poetry Rivals Collection 2009

Mummy and I performed a Burns talk together, "The Immortal Memory" having co-written the script. I remember that day, and how very ill she was. Nevertheless she put on her frock coat and her tartan plaidie and we did quite a double act! Mummy read "My Heart's in the Highlands" and we later recorded it for BBC School radio. I remember hearing her voice on the microphone and thinking how frail she was becoming, but her rendition was quite moving. So Burns was a big part of her life.

An Ode to Burns

He was a dirt poor Laddie toiling the soil,
And living In deep poverty.
He became the Bard
Of Scotland.

A humble, good, education can transform a life.
It transported Burns' life from his Ayrshire roots
To the sophisticated Adams' soirees
In Edinburgh.

His work was adored; overwhelming the ladies.
He was a fisher of men, who showed the way.
He brought a sense of purpose to all who heard
His poetry.

He worked too hard, became very ill,
And was lost to us
At an early age.
The memory of him is burnishing
Strong and true.

An abundance of love poems
Filled his books
To the joy of all.
He was "Aye in love"
Was Burns.

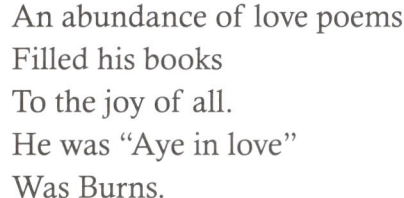

He showed his love for mankind.
Every man was Equal:
Lord, King and Ploughman.
"A man's a man for a' that"!

His poetry lives on
Powerful and true,
And brings Joy
Into our hearts
When ever we hear it
Performed.

"Season of mists and mellow fruitfulness"
KEATS

Mummy used to love being cosy by the fire, she adored the colours of Autumn, and her favourite clothes were often cosy cashmere golds, chestnut browns and creams. Three of her daughters were born in November, so maybe that has something to do with it too! I don't know when she wrote this, but I think it was a later poem of hers. It's very simple but encompasses so much of Keats's "Ode to Autumn" - a poem she loved and often recited to me as a child. When she was evacuated to "Greenhill Lodge" in the Scottish Borders in World War II, she called one of woods "Witchy Wood", maybe that's where she is sitting in her imagination here.

Autumn Sunshine

A soft wind wafts around me
As I sit in the dark, deep wood
Allowing the gentle sun's shafts of light
To surround me and sooth me.
The trees around me are nearly ready
To let fall their precious load.
The earth lies calm under my feet,
Soft and warm and aglow,
Waiting for the rush of autumn storms
And the heavy falls of snow.

Standing by the side of Loch Lomond, such an amazing sight, misty yet shinning on a late Autumn day. To me it was always an oasis of calm in a turbulent world. I love the countryside and spent my childhood in the Scottish Borders. My school, The Rudolf Steiner, was rapidly evacuated from Edinburgh to a beautiful old Hunting Lodge owned by the Duke of Roxburghe. It was called "Greenhill". I was deep in the Cheviot Hills when the first bomb was dropped on the Forth Bridge. It was in those hills that I met a wonderful Gillie (the Duke's gamekeeper) who showed me how to look at nature and cherish it.

The Promise

By the waters of Loch Lomond
Such a moment to remember….
I stared on with such sheer delight
One morning in November.

The mists rose in a pearly hue
To cloud the mountain steep,
And trees around the loch side
Dipped into waters grey and deep.
A silent swan glided by
Just sailing in her sleep.

The morning mists turned into rain
And yet the sun appeared.
Great shafts of light bleached the sky,
And swiftly disappeared.

Still frail, some pale-washed colours
Arched into a fiery bow.
A bridge set in the Heavens
Simply just to show
That God is near us every day,
And wants us all to know.

He walked with me
By those waters deep
That morning in November
I always shall remember.

Written January 2002

Searching through Mummy's papers, after she died, I came across a wrinkled scrap with a half written poem on it. So often when mummy created a poem, she would write it on a scrap of paper, her writing was often so poor, she would sometimes even struggle to read it back herself! She would always ask me to type it up for her and we would often re-work it together. Latterly, she would ring me and dictate the words over the phone. It didn't matter what I was doing at the time, I had to drop everything for the poem! So it seems only right, that this small fragment which I have shaped should be included in this book. Water is a recurring theme throughout Mummy's writing. My husband and I drove up from Loch Lomond through the Trossachs to take these pictures. There is something very simple and beautiful in the picture she paints. I love the image of the fish!

Living Water

Living water, rushing water
Water deep and green and free.
Escalating from great heights,
Surging, dashing for the sea.

Cool water, clear water,
Dropping slow and blue and free
Tinkling gently as it trembles
Till it murmurs to the sea.

Cool water, living water,
Shining bright with golden shimmer
Dropping deep into a pool
Shadowed fish, in sunlight glimmer
Watching still and silent
In living water cool.

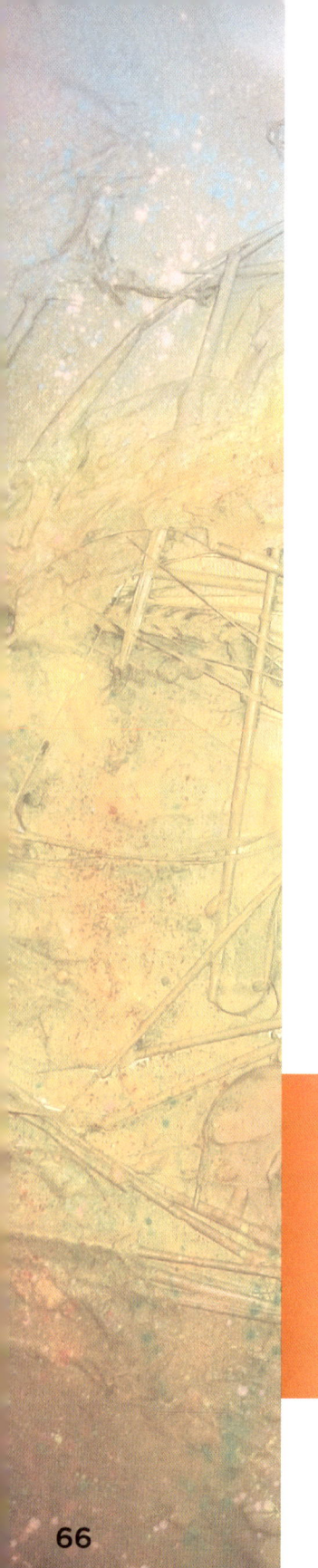

Matthew, my grandson, was moving to the Border Country so that he could attend the Royal Blind School in Edinburgh. His Mother and Father hunted everywhere to find a suitable home for the wee lad to live in. Eventually they found a house that was being built and wanted Grandma and Popsi to come to Scotland to see it before the deal was concluded.

It was a Friday. We left after my dialysis in St. Albans and hit every delay imaginable on the M1! We drove until it became dark, through thunder, rain and terrible winds. Eventually we reached a small village where we lay down our weary heads in the "Black Bull". To celebrate our arrival, we enjoyed French champagne and a tasty meal together. The next morning the skies were clear, the sun was bright above our heads, and we saw Matthew's golden house for the very first time.

I have a powerful memory of Mummy reading this poem aloud to Matthew. It was one of her few trips to our new Scottish home. We held a party to thank all the builders for all the work they had completed. Mummy read this aloud in front of all the guests. She was sitting close to Matthew as she did so. Matthew laughed on cue in verse 2, and Mummy was very moved by this. It was a moment in time I won't ever forget.

I Had a Dream

Look a rainbow!
There's the sun
From the dark
A day begun.
Rushing wind that fills the sky,
We're flying free,
We've got to fly!
To find a house upon a hill
A golden house
A windowsill
A balcony
A great oak door!
And who on earth is this house for?

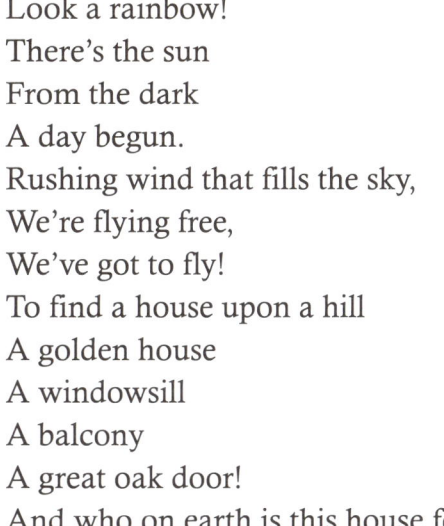

A certain boy with longing eyes,
A smile of heaven that reaches skies,
A boy of wonder and surprise.
Such a story there to tell
A journey straight from heaven to hell.

We're nearly there now,
Yes nearly there.
Only joy now
No despair.
The rawness ending,
The journey too.
A golden house
Is waiting for you,
Our lovely child – MATTHEW!

Written on return from the Scottish Borders
September 25th 2006

One family holiday, we were driving with the grandchildren through Glencoe, the mists were hanging around the mountains, and in one moment we all looked up and saw a lone piper standing on the steep hillside of this valley of death.

The massacre of Glencoe is infamous in Scottish history. On 13th February 1692, 38 members of the Clan MacDonald of Glencoe were killed and subsequently another 40 women and children died of exposure after their homes were burned down. The pibroch is a highland bagpipe often used by clan pipers to play a lament.

Lonely Piper

I saw a man upon a hill, a pibroch in his hand,
The raw, mournful drone sank into the mist,
Dark rock and silver sand.

He stood a sentinel, stark and clear,
A guardian of the glen to
Where the Clans were murdered,
By ugly, senseless men.

They came in kilts and plaidies
And mounted the glens up high.
The battle raged and raged,
Blood peppering the sodden sky.

Too many Scots died that terrible night
Their cries echoed harsh and shrill.
Both Campbells and Macdonalds.
Their clansmen mourn them still.

The piper played his mournful tune
In that grey valley deep,
For the bonny Highland men
Now so silently asleep.

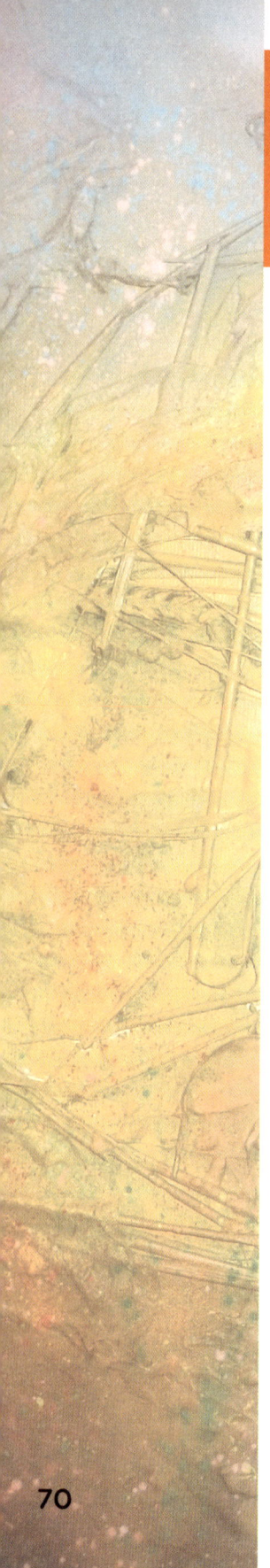

At times all of us, have challenges and extreme difficulties to face. This early poem, demonstrates Mummy's attitude. She didn't believe in wallowing in sadness, she believed in facing challenges even when it was a daily struggle, as it was for her towards the end of her life. It is a dark poem that offers hope.

The Lost Child

Anna is grieving but Anna is brave
Anna is reaching up out of the grave.
For her life, which is shattered
And so sadly broken.
Yet so much inside her
Cries out to be spoken.

She is hurting and silent, and fused to her sorrow
Unable to cope with each day – or the 'morrow.
The toughness, the turmoil, each morning - it's there.
Poor Anna, sad Anna, do not despair
Now listen my child and heed what I say:

"Each morning,
Lean your arms awhile upon the window sill of Heaven
And gaze into the eyes of your Lord,
With this single thought in your mind,
Become strong and step into the day."

This little one was written somewhere
And within your own silence
He is there, always there.

So let him lift you high upon his broad shoulder.
Hold tight little one
He will make you much bolder.
He will kiss your blue eyes into sleep.
He will wake you each morning from renewed slumbers deep.

But most of all Anna,
Discover anew,
The person within you, that is deep and is true.
Love yourself again dear child
For he does adore,
Find yourself again, lost child
And wonder no more.

Come down sweet rain
From heaven above
Refresh her arid soul with love.

Allow him in and flower anew.
Come woman, come Mother, for it is you.
You're not immortal, you're not divine.
Come Mother Earth and drink deep his wine.

Mummy wrote this when we were both part of the Poetry Power group. I remember her telling us, that she had a dream about a mermaid and woke in the night, to write this down. It was a complete departure in style from anything she'd previously written, but I find the eerie imagery of the mermaid's song very powerful.

Tangle and Hair

"Tangle and hair we'll weave thee
Fast to the rock we'll weave thee."

Voices pale with reedy breath,
The mermaids were entwining me fast
Into reed and into sand, rock and long sea grass.

"Tangle and hair we'll weave thee
Fast to the rock we'll weave thee."

The chorus was there again, full of chill
With fairies that come out of the deep
Pulling, pulling, pulling me down
Into a watery sleep.

"Tangle and hair we'll weave thee
Fast to the rock we'll weave thee."

Slimy sea tendrils slid round my neck,
The water rose higher and higher,
The weeds slithered and snaked in my hair
Would I ever escape the Mermaid's Lair?

The water was icy around me now,
Frothing and wild as the sky
Bound to the rock, entwined in weed
Was I really going to die?

"Tangle and hair we'll weave thee
Fast to the rock we'll weave thee."

The voices were fading, fading now fast,
Still calling, calling my name.
Pulling, pulling, pulling me down
Into a deep sea plain.

In a startling moment I awoke.
The bath was awash, pouring water onto the floor,
My hair was entangled in the taps
And my body was cramped and sore.

I eased myself carefully out of the bath
Thank God I was free at last,
But the sea idyll still haunted my brain
An icy nightmare from the past.

"Tangle and hair we'll weave thee
Fast to the rock we'll weave thee."

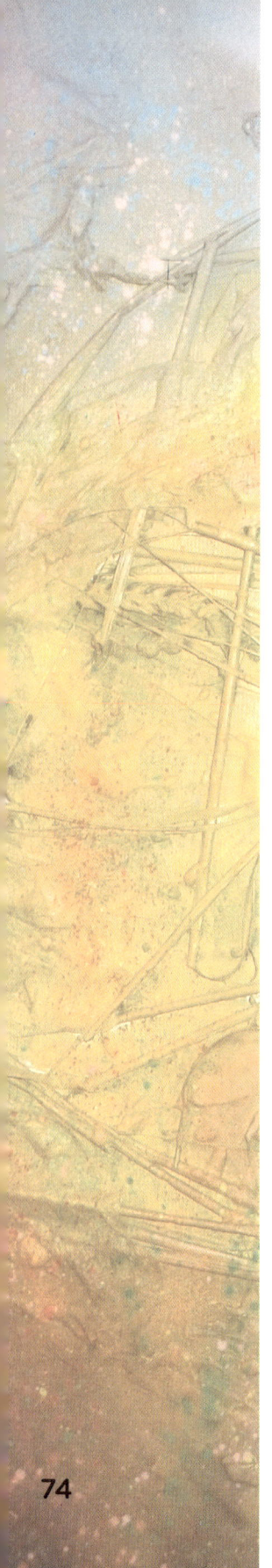

We were living in Northern Ireland in the early 60s. We had two lovely daughters and I was expecting my third child, which I decided to have at home. We had just moved into our new house on the Friday, and on Sunday the midwife was called, and starting chatting away to the baby still waiting to be born. Eventually I was rushed into hospital and three days later, two double breech golden baby girls arrived to fill my arms. In one push we outgrew our income, and the house that we had just built!

My husband was in complete shock. He rang the hospital to speak to the Sister – "But there are no twins in our family" my demented husband said down the phone.

"Well, it's like this Mr. MacEwan", said Sister, "There are now"!

The Burning Seed

My new baby she is coming
And she's just a breath away,
And she's turning like a swimmer
Headed for her own Birthday.

In the arms of my beloved
His strong hands are holding on
Oh sweet Jesus give me strength now!
Make me strong, make me strong!

There are waves upon the seashore,
That tear the sand away,
And another wave is breaking
Help it stay, help it stay.

Dear God, I think I'm drowning
Sharp and quick my babe is crowning,
Help me bear this joy within me
Loving hands and hearts so near,
Help me lover, dearest darling
Help me Mother dearest dear.

There is thunder on the mountain
There is music in the valley
There is tenderness, no trouble
And sweet voices singing clear.

Shooting star, I'm on the ceiling
Christ I'm bursting, bells are pealing
And ten tons of red hot apples
Are now burning to appear.

Stop the music, switch the lights on
Sound the trumpet, I am ready,
She is coming, he is coming
We are bearing down all three.

There was one and then another,
First a girl and then her sister,
A new family were together
Sing a Sanctus joyfully.

On 15th November 1962, the identical twins were born. Mummy wrote this poem to celebrate their 40th Birthday and of course in her usual flamboyant style, she read it out loud to all the guests at the party!

My Golden Girls

You swung on the moon
You leapt on a star
You dropped from afar
Right into my lap.
So alive were these babes
You needed no slap.
You screamed into life
Scorpios, strong, long and golden
You took my breath away,
And still you do, to this very day.

You are the rushing of a fiery sun,
You are the cool of a gentle moon at night,
You are the wind in my hair,
A hurricane.
But I am constantly aware
Of your passion for life.
You found gold in the rainbow
Little blond treasures,
Your children were there.

You have husbands who try to keep up with your pace
You give all of yourselves to your family and friends.
Every day you help someone in the human race.
So where did you come from babies dear?
Out of the everywhere into the here.
Where did you get those eyes so blue?
Out of the sky as you came through.

Rosalind and Andrea what more can I say?
But precious darlings,
Thank you for falling from that star
Because that is exactly what you both are.
Happy 40th Birthday!

Written November 2002

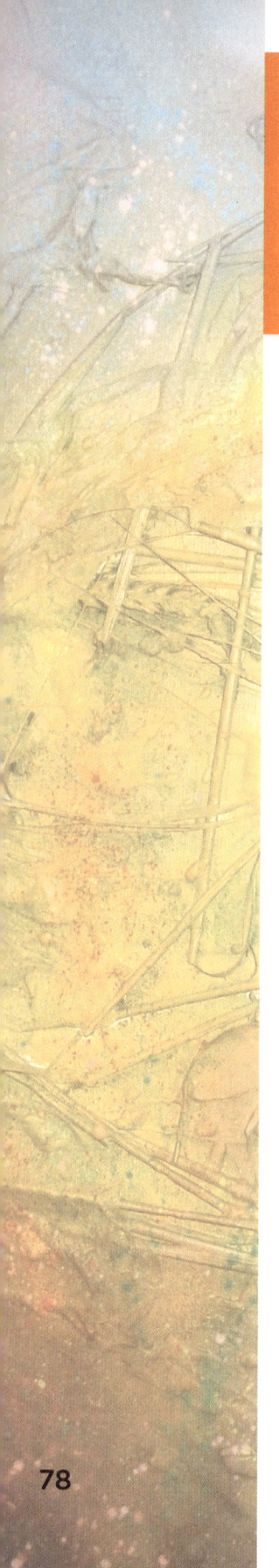

When Mummy first began writing, a helpful technique was to use a picture as a stimulus to create a poem. She wrote this one based on a beautiful pre-Raphaelite portrait of a woman called "Vanity". A copy of the original painting can be found easily online. Mummy so loved the pre-Raphaelite era and I suspect she found this image in one of the lovely art books that adorned the coffee table in her sitting room.

Vanity

How do I see you perfect one?

So haughty and so proud.

Your gentle skin warmed by the sun

Your eyes set wide apart.

You look at me with such disdain,

Did someone break your heart?

Your lips like cherries bright

Do almost give a smile.

Your crown and hair of golden light

Cascade to where your hand

Clasps fast your oval mirror bright.

Bejewelled as desert sand.

Your gown falls around you like

A cloud of green and amber hue,

Entombed with rivulets of gold

And black pearls of morning dew.

Your hands entwined around the beads

Do almost say a prayer.

Do you see what I can see

Or are you just not there?

Written in October 1999
Inspired by "Vanity" the portrait of a woman
by Frank Cadogen Cowper R.A. 1877-1958

winter

> "Farewell to the mountains, high cover'd with snow"
>
> BURNS

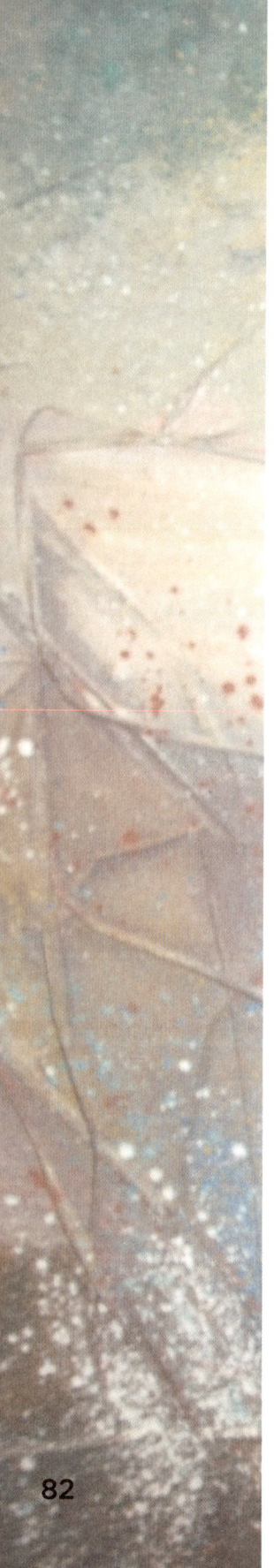

Light

The world is new again,
Untouched, and new again.
Blessed, clean, bright,
White as the first dawn of creation,
The first moment of life.

The world is new again,
Bright, white and new again.
The quiet earth, under our silent footsteps, sleeps,
Weary of its tortured torment.
Silent white and still, hushed
Within its own deep slumbering

Billows of breath before us,
Chill on our faces,
As heart beat to heart beat,
Stride to stride
We silent step into the bright white morning.

The world is new again,
Untouched, and new again.
Cool silence stretches across valleys of white virgin dust.
The bells clear and calling
Suddenly echoing, beckoning
Urging us to draw closer, nearer,
Pulling us laughing, through the drifted snow.

Now we are there.
Warm within the stained glass glow,
Kneeling in the silent light,
We turn to each other, eyes and hearts overflowing.
No need to say that -
The world is new again,
Untouched, white and new again,
Hushed within its own deep slumbering
I walk into my dream and stare.

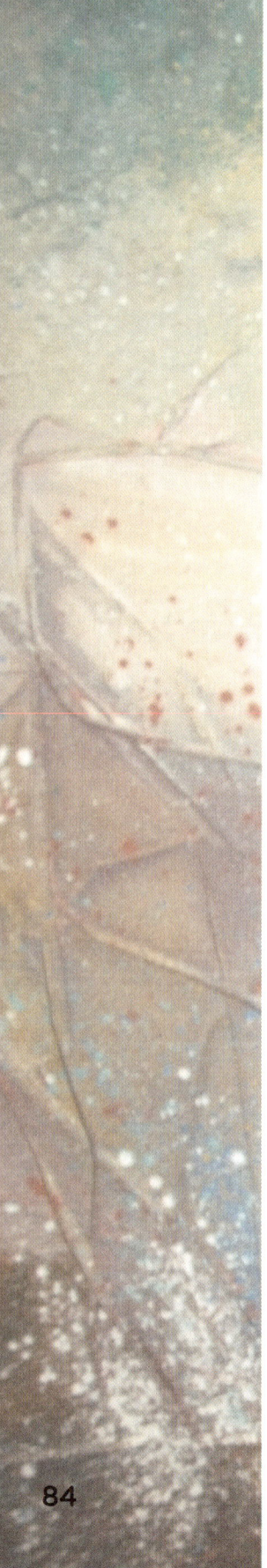

I felt that the story of the birth of Christ could be thought of in a modern way; so Joseph and Mary become "Joe" and "Mari".

A Modern Miracle

It was Christmas Eve
And the snow was deep.
There was silence, not a sound
The car got stuck in a snowdrift
With wheels way up off the ground.

Joe pushed the door open and
Shot into a drift, got up and ran fast to a light,
While Mari crouched down in the car
Trying to keep herself warm
Watching Joe's distant flight.

Suddenly a tall shepherd lifted her up
And carried her away to his farm.
The snow kept falling, white feathered bright
As he brought her inside the barn.

Mari called out:
"The pain it's bad, I can't take any more!"
"Keep strong Mari," Joe urged her. "You really must try".
"It's like red hot apples tearing me apart,
"I'll die, I know that I'll die".

The next moment, there was a great rush of blood,
And a baby began to yell.
Mari held her boy child close in her arms,
Full of newborn smell.

"Don't you worry Lass" the shepherd said,
"Here you'll be safe and sound".
"Put the babe like a lamb in this manger.
I'll lay a blanket for you on the ground".

In the morning Mari woke with a start
"Joe, we've nowhere to lay our head".
"You can live in the cottage just up the lane",
The gentle shepherd said.
"And Joe you can work with the lambs,
There's always too much to do".
There were angels in the air that night
Singing for those special two.

The sky was clear on that Christmas morn
As the dawn began to glow.
The family huddled close round the embers bright,
Snug from the cold and the snow.
Miracles happen every day, well - didn't you know?

Mummy loved to write a poem to commemorate an occasion. I believe she wrote this to celebrate the Christmas meeting of the Poetry Group. She would have certainly read it aloud to great laughter and jollity on that day, and probably with a glass of bubbly in her hand!

Good Friends of Poetry

Good fabulous friends of Poetry!
I wish you all good cheer
And look forward to this Christmas
And then our great New Year!

A time for us to celebrate
Just as we do today
With good friends and such good company
And some with much to say!

So thank you dear Katrina
For good verse and such fine rhyme
As always, it was perfect
Simply just divine!

Now good friends of Poetry
Before Santa comes a-knocking
Make sure you have filled to the brim
Your alliterative, rhyming Christmas stocking!

Written on 9th December 2006

I wrote this piece inspired by Ellen MacArthur's courage and determination to sail her boat "Kingfisher" solo around the world in a race called the Vendeé Globe. Ellen used to call the sea "Neptune" after the Roman water God and would make offerings of food to guarantee a safe voyage. In November 2000 she set off.

She twice had to make emergency repairs during the voyage. To be alone in a dark turbulent sea with icebergs closing around her, she still managed to climb high to mend her mast. This surely tested her courage; but triumphantly she sailed to the end of her amazing journey, joyful and glad. She was the fastest woman to circle the planet when she returned on 11th February 2001 and the youngest competitor ever to finish the race at only age 24.

I was delighted that BBC Schools Radio chose to broadcast my poem, with the wonderful actress Saskia Wickham interpreting my words most beautifully. It was also published in their "Just Poetry" series.

Ellen's Dream

Watch me Neptune I am flying,
Driving, diving down the wave.
Eagle white, swallow bright,
Amazon Kingfisher brave!

Swift and fearless onward skyward
Wings outstretched, wide and tall
See I'm moving through green pastures
Twisting turning through the squall.

Watch me, watch me closely Neptune
As I steer sheer mountains white,
Icy walls which nudge me closer
Floating deep into the night.

Calm and silence all around me
West winds blow me free
Then a crack, a thunder pound,
My wingèd bird falls to the ground.
I'm alone now, not a sound.

Watch me Neptune as I struggle
Climbing high above you now
Mending that poor broken wing
Hanging wounded from the bough.

Watch me Neptune, now I'm surfing
Flying in the joyous race
Wind and rain, sun and spray,
Thrashing at my smiling face.

Triumphantly I turn for home now
Bursting boats, crowds crushing round
Cheering me with such elation
Lifting me up right off the ground.

My childhood dream, my wild sea idyll
"Swallows and Amazons" by my side.
Cutting deep green Neptune waters,
Brave "Kingfisher" as my guide.

The early poetry Group that Mummy belonged to, often used a picture as a stimulus to inspire writing. I don't know exactly which picture of Turner's this was based on, but it seems very apt to follow Ellen's Dream.

Looking at Turner

See a great ship, braving high seas,
Foaming surf around her bow,
Sail of amber lights the skyline,
And she turns her empty prow.

Scudding clouds that merge with sunlight,
Pale horizons meeting dawn,
Rising sun, or is it setting?
Is it evening, is it morn?

Then a great rock cuts the canvas,
Indigo from depths below,
What is hiding in the picture,
Is it friendly, is it foe?

Will the galleon drift forever?
Empty like the Marie Celeste?
Will that gallant gull still follow?
Sunlight on her feathered breast.
Or will the cragged rocks destroy her?
Is she doomed or is she blessed?

Written on being told by my doctor I must not drive any more. My lovely silver car has been sold to one of my dearest friends.

Mummy had a Silver Polo VW car. She loved to drive and would often say her car flew like a bird. It was totally amazing that she managed to drive herself to and from the hospital for dialysis, but eventually she became too unwell to drive anymore. She found this realisation extremely hard. It was only a car, but to Mummy it symbolised so much more.

My Silver Singing Bird

My silver bird has flown away, I cannot find her here.
Where is she hiding, oh where is she hiding?
In a tall tree? I think she's there, yes I can see,
No it's another bird, it lacks the beauty of mine.

Her wings were strong as heavy silk,
With a silver glowing sheen.
She flew with spirit and with speed.
Would she have left, if she had known my need?

Oh silver bird come home to me
And teach me again to fly.
I so loved the air and speed
Driving through the sky.

Oh you broke my heart
And I miss you every day
Come home my lovely and take me fast
Into the meadow to play.

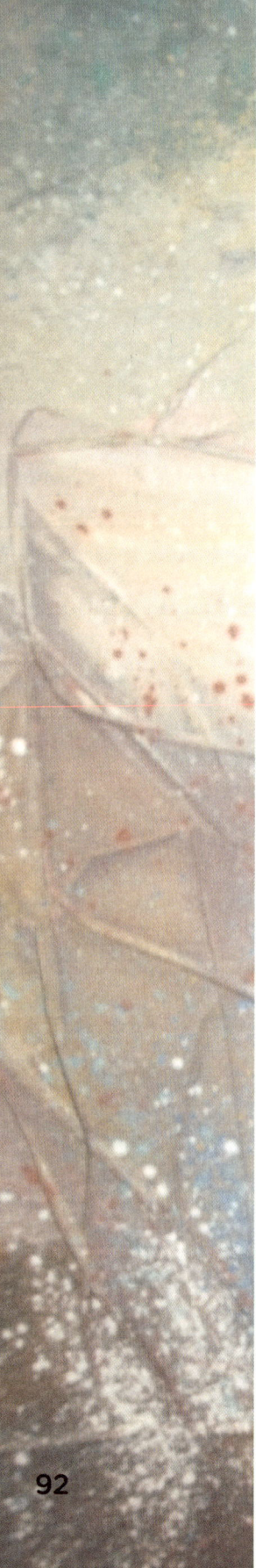

Change

Change, change, change, change
A fresh and new born world.
Spring, Summer, Autumn
New green changes to coppery gold,
As tiny leaves are unfurled.

Change, change, change, change
The world is white and cold.
A child is born one minute
And then they are growing old.
The road is dark and difficult
Next day the road is clear.

Change, change, change, change
Now you can climb the mountain
Without having so much fear.
Pain, pain, take a pill.
You are feeling great, you are feeling ill.
Have you tried just lying down
And keeping really still?

Change, change, change, change
From birth we grow and grow
We learn, we thrive, we stay alive,
But fail to understand
That God is with us, each changing day
And holding tight our hand.

Greed

Greed is the fulcrum of the world
The grease of industry, more iron, more steel,
Buildings reaching to the sky.
The giants of industry, their stomachs brimming,
Their glasses full, their banks overflowing.

More, more, just give me more!
More oil for gold and silver and power.
But still they hunger for more.
Where will the journey take them?
Another pot of gold at the rainbow's end?

But they are on their own, wasted and spent
A lonely grave in waiting
But there is no pocket in the shroud.

Around 6am on Sunday 11th December 2005, I woke up suddenly, ran to the window, looked out – expecting to see a meteorite by the side of the house! I waited, but none of the neighbour's lights went on, so I just thought it was a bad dream. The headline on the BBC News was that there had been an enormous explosion at the Buncefield Oil Terminal in Hemel Hempstead. Despite living 3 miles away, our house shook. So I felt I had to say something about this terrible tragedy. There was no meteorite through the firmament that night, but hundreds of people were left weeping and homeless because their houses had been devastated by this horrendous blast.

Black Sunday

Did you see the sky this morning
Bursting with desire?
Did you hear a strangled train
Screaming from its burrow?
Was that the moment in the day
When you wanted the siren to stop?
Computer chatter, raging their persistent song.
Traffic thunder from the jungle

A thunder crash, a bolt from nowhere!
Black, black, dense driving smoke
Hurtling into the sky.
Filling lungs, filling streets
Filling the air.
What is it? Is this it?
Shock, shock!

Roaring, shooting flames of fire
Tear into the calm morning.
Houses blown apart, families homeless.
Factories gone forever.
Destruction, dirt, rubble
Tears, tears, tears.

Did you see the sky this morning?
Powerful rays defying the blackness.
Strength and light grows with passion
Golden rays defying the clouds,
Darkness falls away to sunshine.
Another day has begun.

Written 27th February 2006

This powerful poem is one of the best I think Mummy ever wrote. It was first published in the St. John's Poetry Group anthology "Tapestry" in 2001. It was later published by Forward Press in their Poets Collection 2008 – Southern England.

Its message about the powers of nature and care for the environment is still as compelling as ever. This was written 4 years before "Black Sunday" and is eerily prophetic.

Earth Sound

Listen to the sound of the earth
The sound of the sea and sky;
The crack of black thunder that echoes
The wing-beat of eagles that fly.
The pounding and crashing of oceans,
The wind that makes waves through the rye.

Listen to the sound of the river
Surging and gushing from its source.
Wait and be still for a moment,
For the stag as he leaps through the gorse.
How blind we've become, how deaf, how dumb,
Not hearing the beat of Earth's sound.

How wondrous is your creation Lord!
How infinite your power!
How selfish we who cannot see
The beauty we devour.
This precious gift, this wondrous earth created for our joy.
Poor baffled, blind and selfish Man,
He only can destroy.

Listen to the sound of the earth,
Take time to stand and stare.
Stop the atomic heartbeat
That trembles and hangs in the air.
Listen feckless, foolish man,
Listen and beware!

My daughter Katriona is Matthew's mother, and I wrote this piece for her. It says everything I wanted to say!

I only found this poem after Mummy died, she left specific instructions it was to be included in this anthology. She had never read or shown it to me in her lifetime. I was quite amazed that she could have written such words about me.

Inspirational

You are inspirational
You lead the way.
You take our hands and
Make our journey easy.

You've come a long way,
From here to eternity and back,
And now the time has come to rest,
To sit in the sun.

You are inspirational.
You speak with such wisdom,
You write with great knowledge.

Now you can watch the mountains.
Let their peace invade your spirit.
Enjoy the wildness of the wind.
Let the skylark lift you to heaven.

You are inspirational,
Beautiful daughter of mine.

I wrote this for Mummy on her Birthday, 7th May 2009. It was the last Birthday we celebrated with her, as she died on 3rd May 2010. I wrote it to encourage her to keep going. Mummy specifically asked it should be included, it seems right it should be the last poem in the book. Her name was beautiful and I dedicate this to her with my deepest love. I have now fulfilled my promise to you Mummy in publishing this book.

Kristin by Katriona

K is for Kristin, not Christine or Kirsty or Kirstin, simply creative Kristin. K is for a kissing embrace, you are all that we love.

R is for reading – you really enjoy words.

I is for interesting – your production ("Sounds Interesting!")

S is for serious strength, for suffering the thundering machine.

T is for tenacity, and for time. You never give up. Your time is now.

I is for your intense creativity. I is for the immortal bard, the immortal word.

N is for nothing will stand in the way of your "joie de vivre". You know how to live life to the full!

K R I S T I N is you.
Each letter makes you everything that you are.

Kristin (Mummy) you are unique, creative, strong, fun and loving.
Enjoy your Birthday in the merry month of May
And CELEBRATE,
For it is never too late to be published!

A Celtic blessing

Deep peace of the pure white moon to you
Deep peace of the pure green grass to you.
Deep peace of the pure brown earth to you
Deep peace of the pure grey dew to you.
Deep peace of the pure blue sky to you.

Deep peace of the running wave to you
Deep peace of the flowing air to you.
Deep peace of the quiet earth to you.
Deep peace of the shining stars to you.
Deep peace of the Son of peace to you.

Traditional

Kristin MacEwan
A short biography

Scottish Roots

Ann Kristin Shirrefs Rainy was born on 7th May 1932 in Alford Aberdeenshire. Kristin was the only child of Elinor and George Theodore Rainy. Elinor's husband was a good deal older than her, and sadly died when Kristin was only 8 months old. So she was brought up solely by her Mother who overcame a great many struggles financially throughout her life.

Kristin was educated at the Rudolf Steiner School in Edinburgh between 1938 and 1950. The Steiner method of learning definitely had a big impact on developing Kristin's creative talents at an early age and firing her imagination. Even when she was 70, she could still recite poems and extracts from Shakespeare that she'd learned as a girl.

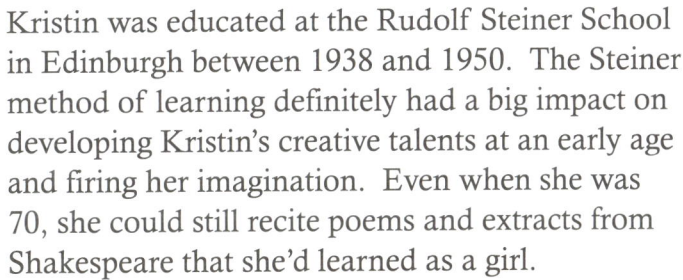

During World War II she was evacuated out of Edinburgh to the Cheviot Hills to a remote place in the Scottish Borders called Hownam. The school moved to "Greenhill", a shooting lodge, owned by the Duke of Roxburghe. Living and learning in such a country environment, had a deep impact on Kristin and her thoughts on life and nature. She even stayed there during the holidays and the Gillie (the gamekeeper for the Roxburgh Estate) taught her "country skills" such as how to guddle a trout, or pluck a pheasant. The experience of nature that Kristin had in the hills at Hownam is reflected a great deal throughout her poetry.

An old exercise book of Kristin's found from those Steiner school days, demonstrates that even as a girl, she was already keen on poetry. This is an extract from it:

"Although we may find it impossible to define poetry, that does not mean that we cannot understand, and enjoy it. This we can do best if we try to stand where the poet stood, at the moment of creation, when his burning desire to embody his vision is most intense. We can only do this with a heightened imagination in which we re-create for ourselves, the pictures he sets before us, and live in them, letting their sounds and colours speak to us."

Kristin's poetry is full of such powerful imagery.

The Arts

In 1950, when just 18, she narrated 11 episodes of a Children's Hour series for BBC Radio Drama produced by Frances Campbell in Edinburgh.

She then attended Atholl Crescent Domestic Science College and gained a Diploma in Institutional Management as well as a Diploma in Dressmaking. She performed at the Edinburgh Footlights Review at the University 2 years running and also attended a modelling course at Edinburgh School of Deportment.

In 1952 she spent a year at Edinburgh University as a non-matriculated student studying singing and the History of Music. During the same period, she went to Art College to study painting, history of art and textile and jewellery design.

In 1953 Kristin moved to Paris for 9 months to study singing and musical interpretation under Pierre Bernac as she had very much wanted to be become an opera singer. Kristin had a most beautiful Mezzo Soprano voice, but in France she discovered that the operatic stage was not for her. Her voice had a powerful tone and her technique was good, but she realised she didn't have the physical stamina required, to live such a demanding and exhausting life.

Returning home and whilst in the process of beginning to train to be an Announcer, she became a member of BBC staff working as a Radio Studio Manager. Between 1954 and 1956, she worked on a wide range of BBC Radio programmes including drama, schools, arts, current affairs and sports reports. Around this time she also spent 3 months doing floral arrangements for the Marine Hotel in North Berwick. Kristin was never formally trained in this art, but she had a natural flair for it, her home was always full of amazing floral decorations. Her talents were often displayed in dramatic designs at the local Church flower festivals.

This coat in forest green has a silver birch fox

Married Life

On 1st June 1956 she married James Duncan MacEwan, a Scottish BBC Television Engineer who came from Prestwick. Kristin and Duncan were deeply in love and it wasn't long before they started a family. Duncan's new job meant a move from Glasgow down to Worcestershire to work at the BBC Engineering training college at Woodnorton Hall.

The early years of their married life were spent in Chipping Camden and later on in Evesham.

Their first child, Fiona was born in 1957, followed by Katriona 18 months later in 1958. Kristin became a very busy homemaker and Mother. Then in 1961, Duncan was promoted to BBC Northern Ireland and the family moved to a rented house for a year whilst their newly designed home was being built in Belfast.

Their undiagnosed identical twins Rosalind and Andrea were born in 1962! By now, Kristin was looking after 4 children under the age of 5½, but she still found time to do some modelling and was involved in compering several fashion shows in Ulster and Eire.

Between 1966 and 1969 Kristin took on the role of Belfast District Commissioner for the Girl Guide Association, she also tested guides and brownies on their various badges such as Entertainer, Singer and Cook. She loved children and enjoyed helping them achieve their full potential.

Being a perfectionist and having high standards meant she didn't pass them on their badges unless they were fully up to scratch!

In 1969, the family moved from Northern Ireland to Hertfordshire. Throughout the 54 years of their very happy marriage, Kristin and Duncan moved house 10 times! They both enjoyed the challenge of all this, and Kristin loved choosing new décor, as she had a tremendous eye for colours and design.

Creative Exploits

By the time the family had settled in Berkhamsted, Hertfordshire, the children were getting older, so Kristin had time to teach singing and speech training to a few students. She remained involved with the guide movement as Chairman of the Local Association. In March 1973 she wrote, produced and directed a large production called "Sounds Interesting", over 450 young people aged 6-19 took part. It made a big impact on the local community and was a huge success.

Between 1976 and 1978 she returned to broadcasting, having been employed by the National Magazine Company in London to record interviews based on articles they were publishing. She contributed to BBC "Woman's hour" and "You and Yours" on Radio 4 and interviewed a wide variety of different people for magazines such as Good Housekeeping, Cosmopolitan and Harpers & Queen. In all, she produced around 80 short radio features across a 2 year period. She enjoyed this stage in her life very much, she was earning again, and it gave her a real feeling of independence.

When the work with National Magazine Company came to an end, Kristin became a designer for a local Interior Design company; she used her creative talents to conceive whole new colour and textile concepts for clients and to follow each project through to completion.

In December 1976 she wrote and directed a Christmas play for young people in the local church; "Berkhamsted to Bethlehem", this was a smaller production than "Sounds Interesting" but still involved just over 100 children!

Kristin was in her element particularly when working on a décor project or writing a script. Now in her early 40s; her children were growing up and she gaining a lot of creative fulfilment especially through her writing.

Just over a year later, she wrote and directed "The Enchanted Garden", a production performed by the whole district of Guides and Brownies in the local area. All Kristin's productions were hugely imaginative and innovative, involving studio recordings of music that had been specially composed, using quadraphonic sound, powerful storytelling, even staging built out of silver birch trees not to mention clouds of dry ice!

In 1998 Kristin and Duncan moved to Hemel Hempstead. At this stage in their lives, the family had all left home and were married with children of their own. Here in Boxmoor, Kristin joined the St. John's Church Poetry group. The monthly meetings meant she had to constantly appear with either a poem she had written, or had to find a published one based on a specific theme. Kristin had always written poetry for special occasions, but this is the key period when her poetry really began to flourish and develop.

Getting Published

In the Spring of 2005, a friend set up a smaller Poetry group and Kristin and her daughter Katriona were asked to join. The group had a specific aim to write as much new material as possible.

The regular meetings of this group of 6 like minded poets were a great stimulus and encouragement to write and read poems aloud together. In 2008, Kristin was thrilled when her poem "Earth Sound" was published by Forward press in "The Poets collection for Southern England." This heralded the beginning half a dozen others being included in future Forward Press anthologies. Seeing a single poem appear in print in a book alongside other poets gave Kristin a tremendous lift, at a time when she became increasingly unwell.

In 2009 Kristin decided she wanted to get all her poetry published herself. She had throughout her entire life, long held a dream to publish her very own book. The novel she said she had inside her, had never come to fruition, but now that she had written around 50 poems, she at last had a body of work. This poetry anthology kept Kristin going spiritually as she became more and more frail, because her kidneys were failing. By this stage, she was unable to concentrate long to read or write, but her mind was still brimming with creative ideas, and she continued to attend the Poetry Group whenever she was well enough. The times of the meetings were even altered to fit in alongside her dialysis pattern and constant visits to hospital.

Kristin had PKD (Polycystic Kidney disease) and was on dialysis as a result of renal failure for the last 8 years of her life.

After a hard fought battle with this illness, Kristin collapsed suddenly at home over the May Bank Holiday weekend and it was clear to all of us, that she didn't have long to live. As she lay dying, she asked me, Katriona (her second daughter) to edit and publish her poetry, and that is the very reason why this book has come into being. On 3rd May 2010 Kristin died peacefully at home, just the way she had wanted.

Kristin, was a highly talented woman who achieved a great many creative things in her life. She was extremely elegant and had a strong presence when she entered a room, she could still turn heads even in her 70s. A few years back, at a Scottish wedding outside Glasgow, she wore a huge straw hat and everyone in the church was asking "Who is that elegant lady?"

She rather enjoyed being at the centre of things. She loved to "hold court" and to talk to people. She loved a party and a glass of bubbly!

I often thought of her as quite an amazing "Diva"! Strangers would sometimes meet her and ask: "are you someone rich and famous?" She was always so glamorous and had the aura of the film star about her!

Kristin was a deeply spiritual person and her Christian faith held strong throughout her life. This is very evident in some of her poetry. It was this faith and belief in God that kept her going when she became so ill. Her strong will and determination was a positive inspiration to all who knew and met her.

The many different coloured threads of her life make a rich and beautiful tapestry. Against the dark threads of her illness are the bright colours of her children and grandchildren, the enduring love of her husband Duncan and her many artistic achievements. Kristin was a creative force and she has left a rich legacy behind in these poems.

I hope that her poetry will give you, the reader time to stand and stare, to reflect and muse, to be uplifted, to have hope and remain positive when life becomes hard, as it did for Kristin. She was a most remarkable woman.

It was her wish that of copy of her book should be available in the waiting area of every dialysis unit in the United Kingdom, and I will endeavour to make that happen.

Thank you Mummy for trusting me to bring your dream to fruition, in getting this, your work published! We have done it at last! How joyful that feels.

by Katriona MacEwan

Poems that inspired and influenced Kristin to write, that you may enjoy reading:

Ode to Autumn by John Keats
The Prelude by William Wordsworth
My Heart's in the Highlands by Robert Burns
The Lake Isle of Innisfree by William Yeats
The Day is Done by Henry Longfellow
Requiescat by Oscar Wild
Rest by Christina Rossetti

Handwritten Poems found in Kristin's Rudolf Steiner Book "My literary Bric-a-brac":

To a Fat Lady Seen From the Train by Frances Cornford
Ducks by F W Harvey
To Sleep by John Keats
An Old Woman of the Roads by Padraic Colum
The Donkey by G.K. Chesterton
The Song of Shadows by Walter de la Mare
Composed upon Westminster Bridge by William Wordsworth
Who Walks With Beauty by David Morton
The Lamb by William Blake
The Grey Squirrel by Humbert Wolfe
The Winds of Fate by Ella Wheeler Wilcox
The Old Woman by Joseph Campbell
When Mary Through the Garden Went by Mary E Coleridge
The Night Has a Thousand Eyes by Francis William Bourdillion
I see His Blood Upon the Rose by Joseph Mary Plunket
Deep Peace of the Running Wave – a Celtic blessing

 PKD Charity is the only charity in the UK dedicated to the concerns of people affected by **Polycystic Kidney Disease** - PKD - a range of inherited, incurable renal conditions.

Their aims are:
- To provide **information, advice and support** to those affected by Polycystic Kidney Disease
- To fund **research** into determining the causes of PKD, discovering treatments and a cure
- To raise **awareness** of PKD, providing information about PKD to patients, the public, the medical community and the media
- www.pkdcharity.org.uk

Acknowledgements

A special thanks to the amazingly talented **Jo Digby**, *north & south design*, for all her patience, kindness and skill in helping me to produce such a beautiful book. I couldn't have done it without you!

Thanks to **Niall McWilliam**, the talented artist who has given permission for me to publish his glorious oil paintings. www.mcwilliam-art.com

Suzi Kennett for her permission in publishing extracts of her artwork of "The Birches".

Thanks to **Mary Bancroft** for her time and kindness spent in typing up the poetry and introductions which Mummy dictated to her.

All photographs used in this anthology have been compiled from the MacEwan family albums. All landscapes are of the Scottish borders and Loch Lomond taken by Katriona MacEwan.